The
POWER
WITHIN
YOU

BOOKS BY JOHN-ROGER

Awakening Into Light
Baraka
Blessings of Light
Buddha Consciousness
The Christ Within
The Consciousness of Soul
A Consciousness of Wealth
Disciples of Christ
Dream Voyages
Drugs
Dynamics of the Lower Self
Inner Worlds of Meditation
The Journey of a Soul
Manual on Using the Light
The Master Chohans of the Color Rays
Passage Into Spirit
The Path to Mastership
Possessions, Projections, and Entities
Sex, Spirit, and You
The Signs of the Times
The Spiritual Family
The Spiritual Promise
The Way Out Book

Available through
BARAKA BOOKS
P.O. Box 3935
Los Angeles, CA 90051

The POWER WITHIN YOU

JOHN-ROGER

I.S.B.N. 0-914829-24-6

First printing 1976
Copyright, © 1976, 1984 by
John-Roger

Revised edition 1984

Printed by Patterson Printing
Benton Harbor, Michigan
United States of America

Published by Baraka Books
P.O. Box 3935, Los Angeles, CA 90051

CONTENTS

ACKNOWLEDGEMENTS

To those dear hearts and skilled artisans who contributed to making this book available, we extend our deep love and appreciation: Pauli McGarry Sanderson, editor of first edition; Ken Thackwell, editor of revised edition; Stede Barber, production and design; Betsy Alexander, copyediting; Ingrid Avallon, design; Muriel Merchant and Holly Duggan, editorial assistants; Vicki Marriott and Maggie Stuhl, production assistants.

CHAPTER I

THE
POWER OF
YOUR
INNER SUCCESS
MECHANISM

There is one God. There is one intellect, which is God's intellect. There is one body, which is God's body. You are a part of God. You are an extension of spiritual energy. We'll call this spiritual energy "universal mind" in order to locate it. You could call it the subconscious mind if you prefer. You can use any word for this energy, as long as you allow your reference points to remain open and to flow freely with the information I will present.

This universal energy is always extended to you. You have the ability, through your conscious mind, to take this energy and work with it. You can use it to build idols to worship or chairs to sit on. You can create happiness or despair from this energy. It doesn't care what its form is because it is essentially formless and universally present.

You can choose the amount of energy you want to use, and you can do with it what you want; you have freedom of choice. There is always a catch, however. The catch is that you will be held responsible for what you create. You will be held responsible for here and now. That's the law. Sometimes we look at that and think, "That means today only. Forget about tomorrow!" So we take great liberties with our creative power. Tomorrow it will be *now* and a year from this point in time it will be *now. Now* is eternity. You are presently in the eternal now of working the energies that are coming to you.

One of the energies that you have present within you is a success mechanism that is (pardon the expression) dying to succeed. It truly wants to get you where you want to go. If you learn to work with it, you will bring success to yourself readily. One of the blocks to success, however, is a lack of understanding of the process of success. To help with this understanding, we're going to use the word *success* as an acronym that will explain some ideas about it.

The first *S* stands for *sincerity*. You must be sincere about where you are going. This means that you must value honesty highly, that you must not abuse or misuse others, and that whatever you do will be of assistance to others. You must not force your ideas upon others. Rather, allow them the opportunity to experience success also.

The *U* stands for *understanding*—understanding the goal toward which you are going. Not only are you sincere in wanting to reach your goal, you also have the understanding of what the goal is.

The first *C* stands for *courage*. This means that when you have said that you want to reach a goal and you understand what you want to reach, then you have the courage to move toward that goal.

The next *C* stands for *charity*. When you reach your goal, it will not be a merely selfish end, but there will be charity for all people. Many people will be able to share in the wealth of your success—not necessarily the financial wealth, but the wealth of your consciousness of success.

The *E* stands for *enthusiasm*. In your enthusiasm, you keep looking toward the goal. Whenever something that could be considered a barrier gets in your way, you reach into the spiritual law of enthusiasm and lift beyond the barrier, or around it, under it, through it—whatever it takes to put you back on the path and to put the goal within reach.

The next *S* stands for *stability*. You must be stable as you move toward your success. Once you say that you are going to do something, follow through with it until it is completed according to what you set out to do. This will produce stability.

The last *S* stands for *satisfaction*. When you reach your goal, you can say, "I am a success." You feel satisfied. This doesn't necessarily mean that you feel whole or complete, but you are able to say, "I did that and I am satisfied with the result. Now I can go on with something else and use what I have learned."

Some of the more sophisticated types of guided missiles are designed to shoot other missiles out of the air. A missile such as this has within it a mechanism that tells it when it is off course. The mechanism doesn't necessarily tell it when it is on course; the missile is just firing and going. When it gets a little off one way or another, however, a built-in feedback mechanism says, "Move a little to the right." It's called negative feedback. The feedback continues until the missile is on target again. When it is on target and close to impact, the part that was keeping it on target shuts off, and other systems are activated as it readies for impact. The guidance system that we have to keep us on the spiritual path while in the physical body is very similar to the mechanism I have just described, and the concept of negative feedback is quite familiar.

If you have an examination coming up tomorrow and you go to a movie tonight, you will start getting negative feedback. Maybe your stomach starts tightening up or you start getting pressure through your back. You might start feeling guilty or nervous. When this happens, people often say, "How awful!" Yet most of us have said, at some time or another, "Lord, just show me the way. If I just had some guidelines, if I could know when I was blowing it and could correct it before I blew it—that would make me so happy!" You have the guidelines. They are already built in. The only requirement is that you become aware enough to recognize the negative feedback for what it is and start moving your consciousness to correct your course.

When you have a decision or a choice coming up, you can turn your attention toward it. In your imagination, make a decision one way or the other. Mentally mock up the results of that decision. Lean into that situation. See it. Feel it. If you get negative feedback, correct the course. In your imagination, make another choice. Repeat the process. See where that decision logically takes you.

You may not be totally accurate in your imaginative mock-ups, but you will probably be close. With a little practice you can become quite accurate. Doing this can help you sort out your possibilities. When you find a decision that produces no negative feedback, that may be the one that is for you. There's no resistance. It's clear. Then your response is simply to move forward.

You might find yourself saying, "I've really felt that something was clear before, only to find myself in a whole lot of trouble." This negative feedback system is sophisticated. It's subtle. There are many variations and changes. From very early childhood, you have been programmed in relation to the environment, and some of this programming you have forgotten. It is still there as an automatic process, however, like reaching out to take hold of things or talking without consciously thinking of the next word. All of these things were learned responses at one time and are now programmed like a computer that goes through a certain routine once it has been activated.

You have to take a close look at what is going on, which areas are consciously directed and which areas are on automatic response. You may find areas you want to redirect so that you can bring them into greater balance with the overall process that you want to accomplish.

The human consciousness is so constructed that you can live with a high degree of pain—physical, emotional, mental, and so on—and live with it for such a long time that you grow accustomed to it. A path filled with accustomed pain may appear to be one of little resistance, so you continue on it for quite some time. You may be feeling the negative feedback that is telling you what is happening, but you are accustomed to it, so you let it go. Then, when it builds to a point of explosion, you say, "But I didn't get any negative feedback." If you take the time to look closely, you will probably see where it was and how you missed it.

Sometimes you become so used to things that you don't notice. You become, in a sense, uncritical in your thinking. Maybe on Monday you agree to meet with someone on Friday. As it gets closer to Friday, you start feeling uncomfortable about the meeting. Since it was agreed upon days ago, you go through with it. As soon as you meet the other person, however, you know the timing is wrong. You think, "Why didn't I cancel this and reschedule it for a better time?" The funny thing is, the other person has probably been feeling the same thing and not saying anything about it either.

It is generally so much better to flow with your inner success mechanism as it gives you feedback. When you do flow with it, your feedback systems will become sharper and more accurate. If you want to become skillful and learn to lift yourself—if you want to become a directed person instead of just being "fired out" and hoping you'll hit the target—then you have to look at your feedback system regularly.

How does the feedback system operate? Sometimes it comes through other people—maybe a raised eyebrow or a slight squint of the eyes at something you say. These actions usually mean to watch out because you may have an argument coming. If you notice the other person's bottom eyelid coming up a bit, you'd better back off from whatever point you're making and change the subject.

You can also throw the ball to the other person by saying, "Now, what was your idea? I'm not sure I got it accurately." This gives the person a chance to present his or her point of view. Then the person no longer feels so threatened by you. Later you have a chance to present your point of view, but it is no longer an argument. It is an exchange, a communication.

If the conversation starts getting a little forceful again, if you start to feel the person tighten up, drop back again. Say, "I'm not sure that I understand your idea clearly. Can you give it to me in different words? Or maybe you could just go over it a little more slowly." That's communication, and it's effective. People give you negative feedback through their responses, and you can turn it around and use it positively to make your communication more effective.

Sometimes negative feedback may come in as irritation from some unknown source. You may say, "I am really irritated!" This may mean that the success mechanism is telling you to back off from the environment for a few moments, come back into yourself, and regain your positive balance. You might want to go to another room, close the door, and re-center yourself. You might take a few moments to look closely at the irritation and see if you can identify the source by looking back over the events of the last few minutes or hours.

For example, if you were feeling centered and flowing ten minutes ago, then Susie came into the room, and now you are feeling irritated, the irritation may be hers. Or it might be in you, a response triggered by her. One way to check it out, if you're unsure, is to ask Susie, "Did you feel irritated with something when you came in just now?" She may tell you she just had a fight with her boss and was very angry with him. Now you know where your irritation came from. If she says, "No, I'm feeling fine," you have to look deeper within yourself to find the cause of the irritation.

You can become quite sharp at working with your negative feedback system. If you become sensitive to it, you'll be able to sense small irritations. If you take the time to confront these situations and clear them at once, you'll probably stop most of the trouble before it ever happens.

While you must observe closely to pick up negative feedback, it's not difficult if you watch for it. There is a sense of well-being that comes with being on target. When you get a bump, this is your feedback mechanism saying, "Watch out. You're getting out of line." It is directing you into a greater awareness of yourself and others. Be open to it and you will find yourself becoming quite adept at dealing with people and directing yourself.

One attitude that can be a great block to your spiritual progress is the one that says, "I'm right. They're wrong!" "They" might be your spouse, your boss, your parents, your children, anyone. That attitude, of course, is immediately observable to "them," and it makes it almost impossible for "them" to communicate effectively with you. This attitude can be extremely subtle. It can affect many areas and cause numerous difficulties.

Have you ever listened to a lecture and thought, "Wow, I wish my husband (or wife) could hear this. This is really meant for them"? That's for you! You may be so busy looking out there at the shortcomings of others that you're missing the messages of your feedback system telling you of your own shortcomings.

There's a technique that will help you get more in tune with yourself and your internal check-and-balance systems. At first it may take a while, but as you become more proficient it will go quickly. Arrange a certain regular time to evaluate the past week. You might choose Sunday nights, for example. Take the time to find a quiet spot where you won't be disturbed, and get comfortable. Then go back in your mind to last Sunday and look at what has happened during the week. Be quite detailed about it. (A good way to do this is to use a spiritual notebook.) Start reviewing the week. Look at where you stepped out of line, with whom you were out of line, what the situations were, and if they resolved themselves. (This same technique is also quite effective on a daily basis.)

A great tendency in the beginning is to lie to yourself. You'll recall a certain situation and quickly think, "Well, that was all their fault, and it wasn't that important anyway," and you'll move right on. If you find yourself wanting to avoid looking at a particular situation, it probably means that it's unclear. If you dismiss an action but find yourself repeatedly thinking about it, it probably isn't clear. If you are clear with a situation, you may not remember it at all, or it may come up just to be reviewed. There won't be much energy with it.

When you feel a force of energy in remembering something, you'd better take a look. Go through the whole week, day by day, looking at what happened. If there are conflicts that are unresolved, find a way to resolve them. Otherwise, the lower levels of consciousness will hang on to those patterns, attempting to clear them in many other ways, and you'll find your energy being scattered. When you have truly cleared these patterns—when you are not holding unresolved conflicts in your consciousness—that is when you will be the most centered and will feel the most creative, dynamic flow of energy within you.

There are several ways to resolve or clear a situation. The best way, if you can do it, is to go to the person with whom you experienced the conflict and clear it consciously. It's easy. You can say, "You know that conversation we had the other day? I thought about it again and wasn't too sure about where we left it. Can you clarify it for me?" The person may say, "Oh, that. You know, I really understood your point of view after I thought about it." Then you can be gracious and say, "That's nice. I really understand where you're coming from, too." So instead of an uneasy relationship, it's now one of harmony and respect. You can release all the tension from your consciousness and be free.

If you get a grade on an exam that you don't think

you deserve, you may resent the teacher but be afraid to ask about it. If you hold the resentment within you, you'll block the flow of energy between you and the teacher. That will make it all the harder to get good grades in the future. Go and discuss the grade with the teacher. Explain what you're feeling and how you see the situation. Rather than change the grade, the teacher may be able to explain how the exam was graded and why you got the grade you did. Ask what you can do to get better grades in the future. Ask the teacher to work with you and help you improve. Communication will open. The teacher will know where you're coming from, and you will probably have a better idea of what's expected of you. The situation will probably be clear.

When you first start evaluating what has happened during each week, you may spend a lot of time talking with people to clear situations and bring understanding to your consciousness. That's all right. It's time well spent. While it's often easy to be honest with other people in telling them where they're wrong, it may hurt to tell yourself where you're wrong. As you continue to confront yourself with situations openly and honestly, however, you will begin to catch your mistakes before they happen. When you know you're wrong, go to the person. If you have apologized to your mother five times already this week and you start to shoot your mouth off again, your negative feedback system will tell you that it's time to make another apology.

You may find that if you can keep your mouth shut, you can bypass the situation. Remember what the negative feedback system is so you can recognize it the next time, too. Maybe your jaw tightens up just before you blow it. Maybe your stomach flutters or your heart beats a little faster. These are signals. Look for them. They're like caution lights. When they go off, drop back quickly and take a conscious look at what's going on. Then, instead of reacting to the situation, direct yourself. You may say, "Maybe we can discuss this later. I really have to be on my way right now." Or you can let the other person be "right"; you can maintain your calm and say, "That's an interesting point of view." Just let it go. There are all sorts of choices.

If you don't have the opportunity to go to a person physically to clear a situation, there are other ways that can clear the imbalance within yourself. If the imbalanced situation was your creation, one way is simply to forgive yourself for your error in consciousness. Send the other person your love and the energy of your Light consciousness, and then send that same love and Light to yourself and forgive yourself for the action. If you truly believe that the situation was the other person's creation, forgive the person and release the hurt, anger, or whatever it is that you are holding on to. Just release it from your consciousness. Don't hang on to it; let it go.

One way to help release it is to use the creative imagination to change your perception of the situation. If it ended with bitter words and hurt feelings, imaginatively change it and see it ending with words of mutual love and respect. See yourself feeling happy and loving toward the other person.

I'm not saying this is easy. Part of the hurt stays with you because the lower self has locked on to the hurt and continually recreates that imagery. If you can effectively change the imagery, the lower self will accept the new image and feel comfortable with it. It will release the hurt, and you will probably forget all about the incident. It may take some practice before this process becomes effective in changing the imagery of certain situations, but keep at it because it can be an excellent tool for releasing blocks from the lower consciousness.

As you continually evaluate your actions— consciously and responsibly—and take the time and effort required to clear imbalanced situations, you will find your life becoming smoother. You'll be in a free consciousness more of the time. You'll have the energy to accomplish more in a positive direction and with greater fulfillment.

One of the biggest blocks to achieving success is having an unrealistic goal. We human beings are goal oriented. Much of a person's depressive state is "I want to go someplace, but I don't know where. I want to do something, but not what I'm doing. I don't know what it is that I really want to do, and if I sound confused, well, that's depressing for me, too!" When people do this to me, I say, "You have to set a goal." They say, "I know, I know. I don't have a goal. How do I get a goal? I ask them what they wish, daydream, or fantasize about or what roles they like to play. They still may say, "I just don't know."

We have all been there. The key is to recognize that there are short-term goals as well as long-term goals. Much of your dissatisfaction and depression comes when you haven't set long-term goals. If you haven't, and that area isn't clear, focus on the short-term goals first and move into success on that level.

What are some examples of short-term goals? They might include washing your clothes, getting things ready for work the next day, going to the market and making sure there's good food available for you and your family, or studying for the next three hours before taking a break. These are all goals. You have to *know* that they are goals. If you say you don't know what you're doing, you've blocked yourself. You do know what you're doing, but you may not have recognized it for what it is.

Goals don't have to be significant to anyone but you. Goals can be simple and straightforward, and they can bring you a lot of happiness, satisfaction, and fulfillment when you look at them for what they are. The process of success is much the same whether you're going toward small goals or big goals. You can practice and become adroit on small successes and then transfer the success mechanism to larger endeavors.

Some women who experience depression or dissatisfaction over their role as housewife or homemaker have not identified the things they do as worthwhile goals. They have opinion wrapped up with fact. The goal of keeping the house clean and getting dinner on the table is every bit as valid as selling $100,000 worth of advertising. It is only opinion that makes one appear more important than the other.

There is a story about a man who lost $200,000 and was totally broke. He was talking with a friend and said, "I am ruined. I am broke. I am disgraced." The friend didn't agree and said, "Well, I understand that you are broke; that's a fact. But that you are ruined or disgraced is your opinion." That way of looking at the situation eliminated all excuses for failure. The man who had lost the money took a good look at himself, went into a different business, made more money than he ever had before, and became even happier in the new job. Much too often, it is not what is actually going on that is the problem, but your opinion *about* it.

People say to me, "I am so lonely, J-R. What can I do about it?" I say, "Tell me what is going on. What are the facts?" They say, "I go to work. I do my work. I don't bother anyone. No one bothers me. I come home, go into my apartment, fix dinner, and sit around and watch TV all by myself. I do this day in and day out. I'm just so lonely." I say, "Now, tell me what is going on there." They say, "I go to work. . . ." I say, "I got all that, but the factual statement is that you are alone. It is your interpretation of being alone that you call 'lonely.' But you could have four people in your apartment and still be lonely." You can say that you are alone, which is a fact, but you can still be happy while you are alone. You can still experience success.

To create your success, you use the creative imagination. On the inner screen of your mind, the theater of your beingness, you set up successful situations. For example, envision yourself walking down a street where there is a crowd. As you move down the street in your consciousness, you may come to a difficult situation. At that moment, you neither retreat nor create pressure. Simply hold there in your mind. Then see yourself comfortably handling the situation. The image of your positive thought will come back through your consciousness and start clearing the pressure at that point. You might have to hold it for quite a while, and you might have to go over this procedure more than once. You may have years of conditioning that you are altering.

As you imaginatively move through the group of people and wish not to feel the phobias that affect your behavior and your relationships with others, imagine yourself surrounded with a beautiful white light. Make the image as beautiful as the most perfect Christmas feeling or Easter spirit or whatever appeals to you. Put that beauty and that love around you. In this theater of your mind, let people relate with you, talk with you, and smile at you. Even more, see yourself smiling back.

You have lied to yourself so often that there is a part of you that figures this is another one of those lies, another one of those betrayals or let-downs. That part within you that has been betrayed before may not cooperate readily. After you have done this envisioning technique a number of times, however, that part will begin to take you seriously, and, at that point, you will start changing. Is this hypnosis? No, because you are not asleep. It is actually high suggestibility. You are suggesting to yourself a positive alternative. It is possibility thinking. You are recognizing that there is a possibility for you to alter patterns that are not working for you.

The whole concept here is one of replacing the imagery that you have been holding against yourself as a block. To replace this imagery of doubt, to see yourself free, to be able to move comfortably wherever you go—this is the path to success.

You can use this theater of the mind to clear illnesses you have in your body if they are psychogenetic or psychic in nature. You envision this part of your beingness, your body, becoming well. You might say, "I don't know what a well liver looks like." If you don't know, get a book to help you with your imaginative process. This process is more than the action of daydreaming. It is more active and more directed in consciousness. You are deliberately imagining those things that you want to come to you. Then you go out into the world to make the outer reality match the inner vision.

There are numerous people who are fearful of success and who continually promote their own failure. It's remarkable, but true. These people might be promoted to high positions in their work; they can work well, achieve degrees of success, and move on to the top. Then, however, they find themselves quitting or getting fired. Or maybe the company goes bankrupt. Something happens that moves them out of that successful level because they can't handle a consciousness of success.

Success is everyone's heritage, however. Potentially, we can have success in everything we do. People ask, "But how can two of us be successful in the same field?" It's easy. One is successful in New York; the other, in California. Can all four billion people on the planet be successful? Yes. Everyone can be successful, each in his or her individual way. If all four billion of us were successful, this place would be heaven on earth. We would be living in the Garden of Eden.

All the great teachers of all times—the adepts, the saviors, the avatars—have come forward and presented the idea that we can envision our divinity and our upliftment. It seems strange that people can come forward with the keys of upliftment and unfoldment, can encourage others to be loving and kind, and can then be called workers of the devil. It also seems strange that they can be accused of being in it for the money, using people, or trying to take over the country. Because of fear, the great leaders are killed, and then people pray to God for help: "Lord, send me a savior. Let me have a teacher, a guru who will enlighten and lift me."

God gives you many teachers, many gurus, many people to lift you and assist you. What about the person you married? What about your children? They are part of your prayer. They are your answer, your teachers sent by God. The answers to your prayers walk toward you all the time. Maybe you pray for a better job, and then the boss fires you. You say, "Oh God, what am I going to do now?" Well, you couldn't get the better job as long as you had this one. Now you are free to get the job you really want.

As an interesting experiment, take a few minutes to write an obituary notice for yourself. If you were to die right now, what would you say about yourself? Could you write something that would be uplifting to another individual? Would you want to write, "I had three cars, a fishing boat, a summer home, and $20,000 in the bank"? Would you write, "I accomplished all the goals I set for myself in my life"? Or "I made my neighborhood a better place in which to live"? Or "I truly loved all my neighbors"? Or "I truly loved my family. I reared my children in a consciousness of love"? What would your obituary be if you were to write it now? Would you be proud of it? It's an interesting exercise. It may give you some insights into where you are and where you are going.

When you have set a goal for yourself—whether it's short-term or long-term—envision yourself getting there. Use your creative imagination and see yourself attaining your goal. That's a good way to stimulate the success mechanism, a good way to prime the pump. Hold the image of your success and your completion in front of you, and keep moving forward. It will become obvious, moment to moment, what must be done next. All you have to do is hold to that completed image of success as your direction and then move to the next obvious thing to be done. That's living in the now, and that's success.

CHAPTER II

THE POWER OF UNIVERSAL MIND

The action of placing something "in the Light" can be interesting. It has brought many things to many people, and people will sometimes receive something they weren't aware they needed. Years ago, a man called me on the phone and said, "John-Roger, I need a job. Will you do what you can to set up a job for me?" I said, "I will place it in the Light for you, and we'll see what happens." A few months later he called back and was upset with me because he hadn't yet gotten a job. He said, "I thought you were the miracle worker. You said you would put it in the Light." I said, "I did. By the way, how is your health?" He said, "That's the only thing that *has* changed. My health is so much better now. I really am healthy." I said, "I think you can get your job now."

About a week later the man called again to say he had a new job. He said, "It's interesting that I could be so stupid and still get such a good job." I said, "It wasn't necessarily stupidity. It was simply not seeing far enough ahead at the time. The important thing is that you can see now." He said, "I couldn't have handled this job if my health hadn't improved. I can see now that the Light brought me greater health to prepare me for this job. If I had gotten it a few months ago, I would have been fired the first or second day. I would have collapsed under the pressure. How can I thank you?" I said, "You might place that thought in the Light for the next person who runs up against a similar situation." He said, "How do I do that?" I said, "I think you have already done it. If you feel strongly enough to call me and express this, I am sure that it is already accomplished."

You can have many things through the universal mind. When you pray repeatedly for something, there is a place in universal mind that hears and answers your prayers. I have traveled into the realm of this creative force many times, and I have seen washers, driers, new cars, new clothing, and things I couldn't have imagined. People have prayed for these things, started the creative process, and then stopped short of getting them. They have gathered and attained the power to bring their desires into manifestation and then stopped—and they were right there! If one thing came to mind when I was seeing these things, it was, "For God's sake, be persistent!" If you aren't, you'll stop short of getting what you want, and then you'll regret not having completed the action.

When you stop before you get what you want, you may get a funny feeling in your body that says, "I feel as if I should be getting something or doing something, but I can't pinpoint what it is. I just don't feel fulfilled." That thing that you have created is yours. You have possessed it mentally, and now you only have to manifest it physically. It might come through the local refrigerator outlet or from your neighbor down the street; everything around you is prepared to bring it in.

Many years ago a friend was trying to sell her home, and we talked about programming the universal mind for what she wanted. She said, "My house isn't selling. It has been on the market for a long time, over six months, without a single good prospect. Will you help me program to sell the house?"

I agreed to show my friend a technique. I asked her to write out everything she wanted to happen with the house. She wrote down the many assets of the house, all its good points, and how beautiful it was. She wrote down all the terms of the sale that she wanted—the price she was asking, the bottom price she would accept, when she wanted it sold, the terms of the financial settlement, interest rates, everything. Then she brought it to me so we could charge the energy together.

I read it over and realized that my friend had also started programming for the person who would buy the house. She had programmed that he would enjoy the house, that he'd be happy there, that he'd be married and have children, and that the family would love the house. Programming these areas was not her concern. Maybe the buyer wouldn't be married, wouldn't have children, and would want to do something entirely different with the property and the house. That would be his right. She was going out of her area of concern. It was valid only to program for selling the house right away and seeing that everyone would benefit from the transaction. Anything else was invalid.

I looked over the programming to make sure everything could work out right, and then we charged it. I suggested that my friend read it over 100 times to activate it in the universal mind. After she had read it about 50 times, she said she no longer knew what the words meant. She had completely lost contact with what was going on, which brought in emotional detachment. After about 75 times, things started coming back into focus, still in a detached way. When she had read it 95 to 100 times, she said, "There was so much power there that it was like God saying those words." The house sold in three weeks. The buyer walked right in the door and said, "I'll take it." It was bought for the right price and at the right interest rate, and everything fell right into line.

There is a key to programming the universal mind that many metaphysicians and science of mind teachers neglect to explain: make sure to write down *every detail*. For the most part, universal mind is a neutral energy. It doesn't have any opinion about or concern with you or your requests. It's just energy. If you're careless and program for something incomplete or foolish, you'll get what you asked for—nothing more, nothing less. These are psychic, magnetic energies you're working with. They're not concerned with any type of judgment or morality. They'll move whatever way you direct them.

I found out the hard way that it is necessary to program very specifically for what you want. Years ago I programmed for a tape recorder. I got one, only to find out that it had only two speeds, and I needed a three-speed machine. So I programmed for one with three speeds. I got one, but it couldn't use seven-inch reels. So I programmed for one with seven-inch reels, got it, and then discovered that what I actually needed was a cassette recorder. I ended up with about 14 tape recorders. I got such good deals on them that I couldn't turn them down. While I could bring them in easily, I needed to learn to program more specifically.

Some people ask or pray or "treat" for something and then let it go. Nothing may happen. Their point of view is that they treated for it; therefore, the treatment will take place. One woman was treating for a tumor. Her treatment was to *deny* that it was there; she was denying its existence. Her technique wasn't working too well because the tumor really was there.

That process is like denying the existence of the chair you are sitting on. When you deny something, you are actually giving energy to it. You know it's real, or you wouldn't be denying it. When you deny something, you actually affirm its existence. That thing will use the energy you give it and grow to a level that you can't handle. *Don't deny it; acknowledge its existence and work to bring it to a level you can handle.*

If you say it's not there, you kid yourself. You lie to yourself and delude yourself. It won't work for you. As soon as you deny something, you know it's real. Holding that denial gives it more energy. Instead of denying, acknowledge that there is an area out of balance, in a state of dis-ease, and then place the Light into it to make it well. Keep sending the Light to that area. Keep visualizing it healed, healthy, and whole. That puts positive energy there; that can heal it.

When you deny something or call it evil, you give power to a negative point of view. In reality, you are Light, and you give Light wherever you place your consciousness. Affirming the existence of something that you want brings it into a vibratory state in the universal mind. If you are satisfied with a vibratory state near you, that's wonderful. Most people want to materialize it to a more physical form, however. To do that, you have to go to an area where you can receive it.

If you want to fish for trout and you see yourself catching a lot of them, don't go into the Sahara and expect the vision to manifest. Go where there is water, where there is a strong possibility of trout. You have to actively place yourself in a position to receive what you want.

Some people sit at home day after day and pray to God for a job. Do they expect somebody to walk up to the door and say, "You're hired"? If you want a job, at least check the want ads. That is one action toward fulfillment. Your next action might be to call someone who is in the area of employment that you want and to see what's available. You could call your friends and say, "I'm looking for a job. Let me know if you hear of any." You have to take action in a positive way. Put the energy out and start pulling to you what you want.

If you want a better job, put the word out. Be specific. "I'd like at least $5,000 more per year. I'd like shorter hours. I'd like to work nearby because I don't want to drive so far. I would like to work with better equipment and have better opportunities for advancement." It is important to be sensible about this. Part of the spiritual path involves your mind, which is the screen of your Soul. Use the mind to see your direction clearly so that you don't go blindly into things.

If you want a new dress, you have to go look for it. You have to put yourself in a position to receive that dress. When you go into the store, the clerk will ask what you're looking for. If you have a clear idea of what you want and begin to describe it, the clerk can catch your vision. She might say, "I think I have just what you want." It saves you time when she can match your vision and say, "Here. How's this?" You say, "Really close. Let me try it on." Maybe it's even better than what you had envisioned, and you take it. You got it because you put yourself in a position to receive it.

You can use the power of the imagination to bring things to you. Universal mind is real. Use the imagination as the key to the door. As soon as the door pops open, step out of the imagination into reality.

The imagination can also create your psychosomatic illnesses, your allergies, your tumors, your decay, and your death. These are aspects of an imagination gone faulty.

Is it faulty to see something as bad? Not necessarily. When you see something that seems bad, that is reality to you; you recognize it as being bad. At this point, you haven't done anything out of line. You are simply recognizing or acknowledging the reality of the moment. While someone else might see it differently, in your consciousness it seems bad. Your next action would be to place the Light into that reality to bring it into balance. That action may make it explode, erupt, clean out—whatever is necessary to bring it back into balance.

If you sit in your chair and say to yourself, "I think those people down the street don't like me, so they're bad people," you are using *negative* imagination. You are building up that image in your mind and creating it. You don't consciously know whether they like you or not. Until you do know, you are simply projecting imagery that may or may not reflect reality.

A husband might say, "My wife's been stepping out; I know it." In his mind, he sees her stepping out on him. Then, when she does, he wonders why. His thought may have created it. Thoughts can be that powerful.

Universal mind doesn't know the concepts of right and wrong. It simply has available energy. It brings you what you envision or imagine (image-in). While everyone has access to this energy, you must learn how to use it to create positive results.

For example, if a woman wants a baby, she can imagine what it is like to have one. She can inwardly experience life with that baby before she even gets pregnant. She does this in her imagination. The husband wants a baby, too, and he also envisions the child. They start talking about the baby they want to have. They talk about the things they want to give it. They give each other a positive vision; they never envision the child being crippled or mentally retarded. They envision it being beautiful, healthy, and perfect. They come into the relationship that brings forth the child. The child is born very beautiful, and they think, "He's just what I wanted, just like I saw him."

There are other factors that can affect the process of universal mind. When you go into universal mind, envision that which you want, and bring it forward, the form can attract Spirit into it. If you envision the child and the vision moves into universal mind, that substance, that essence, moves into a Spirit form and picks out a Soul. In order to work through something, that Soul may bring forward a body with a physical deformity. Then the parent says, "Why me, Lord? Why does this have to happen to me?" There may be karmic situations there for the parents as well as the child.

Depending on the karmic flow, the parents may choose to have the child raised by an institution. Well-meaning friends may judge that and think, "How could they do a thing like that?" They can do it because they are karmically free to do it. The child may have used the parents' bodies simply as a way of getting down to this realm. Then, very soon, the child will go its own way.

In reality, of course, people have karma only with themselves. While people come into close relationships to work through certain karmic situations, the karma is with themselves, not with other people. Other people may help them work out their karma, but it is always their own. Many people may help them fulfill it.

You might ask, "What is my karmic situation with this person?" The karma with *yourself* is that you hurt someone badly in a former lifetime, and now you have to realize that hurt. The person who brings this action to you may or may not have been part of the previous situation. All that matters is that you learn what the infliction is and how to balance the action.

If you are tapping the universal mind and you repeat your program at least 100 times, you will be bringing things to you. If you tap into Spirit, it may manifest through the universal mind. As you repeat your programming, you may think, "How silly. How stupid." Keep going. Many people stop just short of receiving the things for which they are programming.

In essence, this action of programming is a prayer. As you repeat the program, it becomes like a mantra. This mantra builds a force, and the force brings an essence into being within and around you. This essence can be so powerful that when you walk into a store, the salesperson will say, "I know exactly what you are looking for. Come right over here. I have a deal for you. Here it is." You say, "That's it! That's exactly what I wanted."

When you are bringing things forward through programming, get a picture in your mind of what you want. Get a clear *visual* image. Visualizing is vitally important in precipitating things. If you can find an actual picture of what you want, tape it to your mirror or someplace else where you often look. Make it one of the first things you see in the morning and one of the last things you see at night. If you can get a couple of pictures, put them around the house.

If you want to lose weight, put a picture of a slim, attractive person right on the refrigerator door. You will look at that as you go for a snack, and you will turn right around and walk away. That walking away may represent the loss of a pound. If you come back an hour later, that picture will still be right there. Look at it and see yourself being that slim. It will help create that for you.

If you want a new color television, see that television in your front room. See what it will look like and where it will go. See yourself sitting on the couch, watching television in its perfection. Also put on it the price tag you think you can afford. See it being delivered to your house safely, and see it installed correctly. See it all, in complete detail. If you leave something out, you'll miss the perfection. Program it perfectly and place it into universal mind. If you are to get it, the money will appear and you will have it. It will be easy when everything is right and proper. I can't begin to tell you how easy it is when it falls into line.

You may sometimes wonder why you are singled out to have good things come to you. There is no mystery to that. It all follows a logical order of the law. Divine order is everywhere. You might not perceive all its manifestations as divine, however, because you might not know the whole story. You see only the little story from your pigeonhole. You interpret it from one little section of your mind and can't even begin to comprehend the great area beyond your own feelings. Is it any wonder that you can end up in confusion?

Before letting a thought go when programming the universal mind, place it in the Light *for the highest good.* You will find things coming into a greater, more perfect balance around you. Always ask that God's will be done for the highest good. Then if you are to receive something, it comes in balance.

If you can't ask for it that way, you may still get what you asked for, but you may also get everything else that goes with it. You may get the refrigerator you want, but the cooling system breaks down. You get that fixed, and then the motor goes out. You get that fixed, and then the refrigerator develops cracks. You think, "This is more trouble than it's worth."

In addition, when I program for things, I always place out the idea that the money for my requests will become available in a way that causes no harm to anyone. Otherwise, it's possible that the money could come in through a legacy due to someone's death.

Years ago I was looking for a new house. I wanted one where I could do my work effectively, one that would be good for me. I programmed for all the things that I wanted. One of the things I programmed for was a large yard. The first house I saw had a large yard, but there was a drainage problem—the yard flooded during the winter rains. So I programmed for a house with a large yard and good drainage. The next house I found was built right beside a drainage wash for the city. These experiences kept happening. I found that it was becoming almost impossible to think of all the contingencies. I kept leaving things out, and each house I found reflected areas for which I had forgotten to program.

Finally I gave up, placed it in the Light for the highest

good, and said, "Lord, you know what I need more than I do. Whatever you come up with will be fine with me." It wasn't more than a week or so before I found a beautiful house that included all the things I wanted—and much more. It really is helpful to put in that safety clause: for the highest good.

CHAPTER III

THE
POWER
OF YOUR MIND

The mind is a tool for this level, and it brings similar experiences to many people. While some people may experience more mental karma than others, the essential action of the mind is the same with each of us. Do you think you're alone in the things you experience? Check with the people around you.

You may sometimes separate yourself from a person or group because you think they do strange things. Perhaps they do, but let's hear all your thoughts and *then* decide what's strange and what isn't.

You might think, "No way. I'm not going to tell you my inner thoughts; they're weird. Nobody thinks what I think!" Then you talk to your best friend, who says, "You know, sometimes I get these strange thoughts" and then tells you almost exactly what you had been thinking. You think, "Oh Lord, there are two of us!" Then you meet someone else who says, "I've had the strangest thoughts lately." Soon you are forming groups to discuss these shared experiences.

Alcoholics used to think they were all alone in their

experience. Some still do. In Alcoholics Anonymous, however, they come together to lift and assist one another by talking about their inner experiences in relation to alcohol. They find that they have shared many similar experiences. Special chapters of AA have been formed for the spouses and for the children of alcoholics because their experiences are also quite similar.

People who were having psychic or spiritual experiences used to think they were alone. Now, people are coming together in increasing numbers to talk about these areas. They are finding out that many other people are experiencing similar things.

Some people are still frightened of spiritual experiences, thinking they belong in the category of ghost stories and haunted houses. This isn't true. Many things exist outside the range of our physical senses, and we cannot see, feel, taste, or hear them. Spiritual experiences are a normal, matter-of-fact reality. There is nothing abnormal or strange about them.

As the human consciousness expands into Light, it goes into all things. Here on this planet, however, our consciousness is often compacted into the physical form. It seldom pays attention to anything else. At the same time, some part within us says, "I know there's more out there." The part that looks can't see it. The part that listens can't hear it. The part that touches can't feel it. While none of our senses are aware of it, the part of us that is an extension of a greater beingness knows there is more than this physical existence.

In this world today, it seems that there are many causes for fear, insecurity, and despair. For example, some people fear the threatened shortages of food and fuel. Of course, there are shortages. There always have been. There are whole cultures and countries that have never had adequate food, fuel, or housing for their people. The real shortage today, however, is of brains—the ability to look ahead, think, and plan. The other shortages exist only because of the way existing supplies are mishandled, mismanaged, and poorly distributed.

If you have the courage to look ahead realistically and to think and plan intelligently, you have the ability to take care of yourself. How do you handle fear, insecurity, and anger when they come into your consciousness? Go into the theater of the mind and envision yourself being able to think and plan intelligently. Work on it. Practice it.

Have you heard the expression sometimes used to explain why some people are successful? It is that, while other people were sleeping, they were working their way up. It makes you wonder if they ever got sleepy, doesn't it? Perhaps the expression actually means that while other people were asleep in their consciousness, the successful ones were active and alert, looking ahead, thinking, planning, and implementing. They were putting in the correct image of success and accomplishment, and they weren't wasting time. They were actively perfecting their levels of consciousness and becoming positive in their approach to life.

Thinking is not a natural process of the human consciousness. You may say, "Sure it is. Everybody thinks." I have news for you: very few people think. Most people *react* and then pass that off as thinking. Thinking is the *cause* of things. Reaction is the *effect*.

How often are you actually thinking, and how often are you reacting? You are probably reacting about 90 percent of the time. For the most part, you are reacting either to your previous reactions or to someone else's reactions. It's a long chain of effect and effect and effect. It's like dominos: you hit one and they all go.

When you experience negativity, ask yourself if you are negative all the time. The answer, of course, is no. Since you are not negative all the time, negativity is not permanent. You may say, "But I'm not happy all the time, either, so happiness isn't permanent." I never said it was. There is a middle ground, however, where you feel comfortable with what is going on around and within you.

Happiness comes out of the mind, emotions, and body, which are always changing, but joy comes from Spirit. So it's a fact that when you rise to the Spirit of the occasion and truly partake of the Spirit, you have joy—even in the midst of physical, emotional, or mental despair.

Most despair comes from your interpretation of what is going on, not from the fact of what is going on. Only rarely does a true personal catastrophe take place. You can create a consciousness of catastrophe, however, by your interpretation of the facts.

Let's say you are sitting by yourself in a chair. That is a fact. Your interpretation of that fact may be "I'm lonely." When you have awakened to the Spirit within you, you will *know* that you are never alone. You will not feel the loneliness. The Beloved is always with you, always in your company. All you need to do is awaken to that reality.

Have you ever set a goal for yourself, only to find yourself falling short of it? Maybe you have come very close but haven't reached into the success of completion.

Use the theater of the mind to envision your success—your accomplishment, completion, achievement. If you create this vision strongly enough, it will happen for you. Even when a part of you seems to give up—consciously or otherwise—there is another part that will hold the vision. Then, perhaps when you least expect it, you will "suddenly" have accomplished your goal.

Once you have set a goal or direction for yourself, you may experience a fear of failure, a fear of being unable to measure up and reach that goal. You're in good company. I'm sure that everyone on the planet has experienced this fear. There are no real failures, however. The word *failure* is only your interpretation of a test you aren't prepared to handle yet.

Perhaps the reason you aren't prepared to handle it is that you haven't imaged-in enough correct information. You haven't gone over it enough in your mind, placed it in your emotions as confidence, or placed it in your body as a skill that you can produce when the test comes. These so-called failures aren't recorded against you. You can simply say, "Yes, I failed that course. I guess I had better repeat it." Or "I guess I'm not cut out for that. I'll start in another direction."

The test does not record your failure; *you* record your failure. The test records your lack of preparation and reveals to you the work necessary for your success. Understanding this, you may see that your job is to go back, review the material you didn't understand before, and learn it this time. When you can approach life with the attitude that each step is a preparation for the next step, you'll be in good territory.

How would you like it if, on the ladder to heaven,

someone went ahead of you and built each rung perfectly so that you and each succeeding person could go up easily? That would be nice, wouldn't it? How would you like it, however, if the person in front of you couldn't even hammer a nail straight and left the rungs crooked and loose? Would you want to follow that person? You would probably prefer to follow the one who does things right, is careful, and checks their work, and even when you follow such a person, you still must be responsible for your own progression.

While it is wise to follow the best example you can find, it is also wise to check things out for yourself. At each step up the ladder, test to make sure that you are still firmly supported. Watch the step in front of you; make sure it's solid. When it comes toward you, take it, and keep your eyes on it until it is below you. Then watch the next step as it comes. That way, you won't be unsure of the step you're on; you will already have prepared yourself by watchfulness, thoroughness, and constant checking. You won't stumble and fall over your work, and the people below will be able to follow you safely.

When the time is right, you will awaken to the Light consciousness within you. One aspect of your awakening will be assuming responsibility for yourself and your actions. Suppose your neighbor recommends a car, you buy it, and it turns out to be lousy. Whose fault is it? Your neighbor's? No way. It's your fault. Why didn't you check it out? Why didn't you take it to your mechanic? Why didn't you go through it more thoroughly?

The only true answer is simply that you didn't. Don't blame your neighbor, and don't blame yourself. Let the experience be your teacher. Learn from it; it's been a valuable experience. When you get sick and tired of making dumb mistakes, you'll get a little smarter in your approach. I have often said, "When you get sick and tired of being tired and sick, you'll change." It's rare that you'll change prior to that point, however, unless you have someone who loves you enough to push you out of bed in the morning and get you on your way.

It's great to have someone who loves you into a greater perfection in spite of your bad habits. When you burn breakfast, they still come home in the evening. They may express a preference for unburned breakfast, but it's not the end of the world. If you burn it again the next morning, they may decide to skip breakfast. If you burn it the third day, they may decide to fix their own. Perhaps they should fix yours, too. They might be able to teach you something.

Would you believe that I actually met a woman who consistently burned the toast, day after day, and then scraped the black off? It's true. I could hardly believe it. I asked her husband, "Does your wife really cook toast by making sure it's burned on both sides and then scraping it to the color you like?" He said, "How else do you do it?" I could have told him, but why ruin a perfect marriage? There is no need to show people a better way if the way they are doing it, as bad as it may seem, is working for them.

Many years ago, when I was very young, I visited an Indian reservation. I was alien to the Indian culture and didn't know much about Indians or their history. I'd been raised on the stereotypes of "cowboys and Indians," where the Indians were always the bad guys. It was all I knew. I thought Indians were there for the cavalry to kill. That was the conditioning in which I grew up.

When I was on the reservation, I saw some men and women crying because a baby had died. Their grief was profound. It rocked my consciousness to see them cry, just as people from my culture would cry if a child in the family died. I'd thought that we were the only ones with sensitivity. That was a big lesson for me in universal consciousness.

Shortly after that, I visited a section of town in which most of the black people in that area lived. The conditioning of my consciousness had been that black people were somehow radically different from white people. Yet I saw mothers and fathers loving their children and kids playing the same kinds of games I played. I began to realize that *we are all one*, that the human experience is essentially the same for all of us.

Children are too often reared with and taught a consciousness of separation that is entirely inaccurate and damaging. It is good for us all, children and adults alike, to get to know people of many different colors, creeds, and socioeconomic levels and to learn to love all people for the unique individuals they are.

Someone once asked me why I thought God made the different races. I said, "Wouldn't it be boring if we were all one color? It's neat to see all the different colors. It's fantastic. It's a rainbow, a kaleidoscope." The different races represent different experiences on this plane, that's all. All of us experience each of them at one time or another. Understanding this idea can quickly bring us into a oneness.

I think God has done a fine job by putting us here on Earth and saying, "You figure it out; you work it out together." About the time you say, "Not me," Spirit ushers forth shortages that force understanding upon you. Then you say, "There are poor people in other countries; children are cold, hungry, and crying. As bad as it seems here, it's worse there." Your empathy goes out and says, "Let's take care of them."

Whether or not you can do anything physically, start praying for these people. Start holding visions of success for them. Start taking these success images and putting them out, sending these people all the energy you can for their upliftment. If enough people do this, the consciousness will start moving, and greater success will start flowing to those people to whom you are sending this energy.

You were put here with something special inside you: the ability to contact Spirit within. With that spiritual energy, you can contact universal mind and place success images into it through your own mind. When you have done this long enough, your positive images will weigh upon the universal mind, and they will start to precipitate down into reality. To implement these positive images, universal mind chooses people whose minds are open— architects, engineers, scientists, and similar individuals who have within them the creative urge to be open to what is new.

If you find you are not changing, you may be in a rut. Do you know the difference between a rut and a grave? A rut is open at both ends. It's important to keep open so that you can keep moving. If you find yourself boxed in, you may have to leave the body, and your obituary notice may not read the way you would like it to.

Many people say, "I don't care what happens. I don't

believe in reincarnation, and I'm not coming back here."
Are you aware that your beliefs do not determine reality?
For the most part, what takes place here is determined by
what has been imaged in, created, and precipitated down
from universal mind.

Are you aware that if you wish for something, you
will get it? *When* you are going to get it is another matter.
You may have to come back in another lifetime to get it. Be
careful what you wish for. Be careful what you ask for.
You are a creator. You *can* make things appear, so look
ahead and make sure that what you're asking for is what
you truly want.

If you want to play it safe, always ask for the highest
good to take place. That's your insurance policy, your
safety clause. Then, if you don't get something you asked
for, thank God.

If you want something that you can provide for
yourself, don't just ask God for it; go out and work to get
it. Don't ask God to carry your bags if you have two good
arms. God isn't the great bellhop in the sky. Anyway, if
you can order God around, that means *you're* God. If you
can't order God around, it simply means that you're a
smaller god. You are still a god of your own beingness, of
your own inner universe.

What happens in your universe when you're upset,
depressed, and miserable? I suppose you're creating earth-
quakes on your planet. Maybe you're destroying your in-
habitants. Perhaps you are one of the wrathful gods who
rule through fear. Is that the way you want God to be with
you? No, I'm sure you want God to take care of you, be
kind and benevolent, and give you what you need. If that
is so, then perhaps you should watch what you are doing

within your own universe. Universal mind simply hands you a duplicate of your image. In order to receive a positive creation, you must create positively; you can't hold even one negative thought toward your positive image.

I have visited many ashrams around the world. Some were so filthy that when I was invited to sit down I said, "No, I don't think I want to. I don't know what might get up with me." Does that mean that I was so clean that I was above reproach? No, but I'm not blind.

The people in the ashram said, "This is all of God; all of this is God." I said, "I agree. But the sewer is also of God. Why don't you sit in the sewer?" They said, "You don't have to do that to know that God is there, also." I said, "Right, and you don't have to sit in filth here either. By the way, how is the health of the people living here?" They said, "We've had a lot of illness lately." I said, "It's the food that you're feeding them. You aren't taking care of your people." They said, "But it's natural food." I said, "That's true, but that's no reason to prepare it in a filthy way."

If there isn't practicality in your spiritual approach, what good is it on this level? What good is it to be so spiritual and uplifted that you won't empty the garbage or take a shower?

It is by your work that you are known, by your emotions that you are loved, and by your thoughts that you are respected. That doesn't have a lot to do with the Soul, however, because the Soul is already perfect. You might ask, "If the Soul is already perfect, what is it doing here?" It is bringing perfection to this level. It is bringing the golden age of God consciousness to this level of existence.

Your job is to awaken the levels inside you that are asleep, to awaken to the consciousness of love, Light, and Sound.

As this consciousness comes into the mind, you will say, "I understand." You may awaken slowly to this consciousness of Light. It may take some time before it makes sense to the mind, longer yet before it gets into the emotions so that you begin to feel good about it, and even longer to get into the body so that you are motivated physically.

Each person's spiritual progression is also highly individual. Some people may feel emotionally comfortable with the Light long before it makes sense to them mentally. Some people may fight it both mentally and emotionally while they keep coming back for more. It happens how it happens. Don't set up conditions or expectations for yourself. Just let it be.

CHAPTER IV

THE
POWER OF
YOUR
SUBCONSCIOUS

Your subconscious mind is a powerful force within your consciousness. Some people try to deny its expression, some give in to it, and others are simply ignorant of it. When you can learn to work in harmony and cooperation with your subconscious, you can bring your expression into greater balance.

The power of the subconscious is tremendous. There are few things that can stand against it. It has wisdom, knowledge, and a beautiful ability to find its way through all the obstacles that are placed in front of it. It will sidestep adversities and forge ahead when there are opportunities.

When you come into contact with others, there will often be communication and interaction between the subconscious minds. There may be subconscious attempts to control one another. Deceit can function within these areas of control.

At times you may express emotional deceit. When someone asks, "Do you love me?" and you say yes, even though you aren't loving them at that particular time, that's deceit.

You might wonder if it would be wiser to tell the truth, knowing it will upset them, than to say the lie, knowing you will love them later on. I think that when you tell someone you love them and you don't, they know you don't. They may respect you more if you honestly say, "No, right now I don't love you. I think you're the biggest stinker in the whole world. But give me 20 minutes to work on this. I loved you before, and I'm sure that when I get over this irritation, I'll love you again." That's being honest.

There is also deceit of the intellect. Some people will say they know some particular skill in order to get a job. If they don't have that skill, they are entering into deceit, and it will catch up with them.

There is deceit of the subconscious mind as well. This is like deceiving yourself. You say, "Yes, I enjoyed spending the evening with you," but the subconscious says, "I didn't. And it will be a long time before I go out with you again!"

The subconscious appears to have a mind of its own. You should learn to cooperate with it, work with it, direct it, and educate it. If you are deceiving it, you may start on a path of endeavor only to find yourself backing off rapidly because you sense no support from your subconscious.

If the conscious mind is in the habit of starting one project after another without completing any of them, the subconscious may be attempting to complete each unfinished project in order to fulfill that which has been started. Without the cooperation of the conscious mind, however, the subconscious can neither accomplish nor complete anything. It will feel betrayed and deceived.

It is important not to have too many irons in the fire. The subconscious will have trouble handling that situation. Complete the projects you begin, fulfill the commitments you have made, live up to the promises you have made. Then both your subconscious and your conscious self can have success, which leads to a feeling of fulfillment and worthiness.

When you are true to yourself, your subconscious mind can also be true. Your conscious self, as master of the household, reaches down to the subconscious mind and lifts it up. Then both subconscious and conscious can move into the higher expression and function together as a unit for greater balance and completion.

We humans are to have joy everlasting, and we are also held responsible for our creations. This responsibility has led some people to say, "In that case, I'll just sit by and do nothing." This approach is as much an active creation as any other, however. Decisions will be made for you—by default—if you don't make them for yourself.

Unless you make the decision to learn from what you are doing, you cannot expect to receive the greater action of Spirit as it comes forward. There are great blessings being showered on the earth at every moment. If you say, "I'm just waiting for the right moment to appear," the right moment will come and go even as you are speaking those words. You deceive yourself if you think otherwise. You must step into cooperation and learn to work with yourself to bring to yourself greater abilities, greater realizations, and greater enlightenment.

Ultimately, whom can you deceive? Only yourself. You may deceive others temporarily, but they will discover the truth soon enough. It's fairly easy to forgive the deceits of the mind and emotions, for these occur for many reasons. Similarly, we can forgive the deceits between the conscious and the subconscious minds. It may be more difficult, however, to forgive the deceits of one heart to another.

When you have committed the totality of your be-ingness to another person, can you draw back? No, it really must be "full steam ahead." While the things you are working through now may appear as turmoil, desperation, and heartache, they are actually your joy and happiness tomorrow. The depth to which you feel your despair and agony is the depth to which you will feel your joy and harmony. When despair comes to your doorstep, joy is there, also.

We sometimes wonder at the sadness of parting. The sadness is simply saying that we will miss all the joy and gladness that we shared together. We often make our condition worse in our minds than it could ever be in reality. You may have wondered, "Dear God, how am I going to get through this?" Through *this?* What is *this?* You're still here, so whatever *this* was, you got through it. You placed far more importance on your catastrophes than they were worth.

If your parents were wise, they taught you many things and gave you many keys for living. They disciplined you, explained things to you, and showed you the results of your actions. This is part of the education of the con-sciousness. Too often, however, parents educate their children through some sort of punishment. If you did what they told you not to do, you were punished. That punish-ment locked into the lower mind, the subconscious mind. It locked in because of the irritation and pain. These locks in your subconscious equate the pain with everything that was around you at the time the incident took place.

Let's say you're riding in the car with your spouse and you both want to go to different movies. In the process of deciding, whoever demonstrates a greater energy level wins. The one who loses, however, may lock patterns of hurt and resentment into the subconscious mind.

The one who loses might say, "Why can't we ever do what *I* want to do? Why do we always have to do what *you* want to do?" That is the first step in psychic or emotional blackmail. Then they might continue, "This show is too expensive; the other one is cheaper. We can't afford this." Now money has become part of the issue as well. By the time you pull into the parking lot, a family quarrel is raging. At this point, one or both of you might feel like saying, "You go to the movie you want, and I'll go to the movie I want!"

Let's say that, as all this is going on, it is raining and you are hearing the windshield wipers and the song on the radio and, as you pull into the parking lot (and the argument is at its peak), the parking attendant comes up and gives you a yellow ticket to pick your car up after the show. Your subconscious mind is recording all of this accurately and in precise detail. It really doesn't matter which movie you go to at this point because the damage has already been done. You have locked the pain into the subconscious mind.

Six years later, someone may hand you a yellow ticket of some sort, and you will experience a burst of irritation and resentment toward that person. The subconscious mind will not differentiate this incident from the one that happened six years ago. You'll say, "I don't like that person, and I don't know why. It's the first time I've ever seen him, yet he really irritates me." You're not even aware that it's the yellow piece of paper that has triggered your response.

The subconscious mind makes all things equal. The fight with your spouse is equated with the rain, the windshield wipers, the song on the radio, the parking attendant, and the yellow slip of paper. The subconscious does not separate or differentiate.

At this point you can get locked in with negative energy. If you promote an action of irritation against this new person, you then become responsible for that. Another detail may become associated with the new pain, and the pattern will be reinforced. It is very difficult to break these patterns, to lift them into a positive expression. You may have to suffer the pain of the subconscious even as you are reaching into Spirit.

Eight years later you may hear the same song that you heard on the night of the argument, and you may experience an acute irritation. You may have a fight with your spouse and wonder why it's happening. Your subconscious is saying, "This is the same fight we had before."

You may find yourself hung up on windshield wipers, always checking the blades to see if they're working. The concern has been locked in by these associative patterns in what we call the "reactive mind." The floor plan is laid.

These subconscious blocks can produce illness and economic distress. The subconscious will throw up visions of poverty, and you'll fear that everybody is going to starve to death. When people are worried about famines, famines take place.

You can take the energy of the subconscious and use it through the universal mind to unlock supply. Spirit is infinitely supplying. You have a silent, secret partner called universal mind. It works quietly and diligently to fulfill your destiny by the best route and in the best direction possible based upon who you are, what you have to work with, and what you have done in the past. The plan is laid out perfectly for you. All you have to do is walk through it.

Some people are chronic worriers. They say, "I worry all the time. I can't stop worrying." I ask, "Does that do anything for you?" They say, "No, but somebody has to worry." Is that true? Does somebody have to worry? I don't think so. I can understand having concern and doing what you can in a situation and, with what you can't do, saying, "Lord, it's yours. It's beyond my ability." In your subconscious, however, you may have conditioned energy that says, "I *should* be able to do something." So you may take on a responsibility that you can't handle and then collapse and record failure against yourself.

There is no trouble when the subconscious records in the positive. Everything is happy and wonderful. There is no need even to be concerned with the subconscious; everything is joyful. To achieve that clarity, however, you have to release the last bit of negative energy that is locked away.

How can you work with spiritual energy when your subconscious has already been conditioned into certain patterns? There is a great key for releasing and changing subconscious blocks. It has been presented by all the great spiritual teachers of all times. It is this: "With enough loving, everything is made new." That is a fantastic statement. If it is true, if the great teachers were prophetic, then you can fulfill their prophecy.

The timing is up to you. There is no urgency in Spirit; it will be here tomorrow and tomorrow and tomorrow. It is always here and eternally now. In reality there is no urgency. The urgency you experience is yours as an individual, a personality. You may want to watch, therefore, that you don't mess up a good work by overreacting when you could be self-directing and productive. You don't have to breathe tomorrow's air tonight. You can take it easy. That's one of the keys to breaking these blocks.

Take some time to sit back in a chair comfortably. Relax the pressure in your physical body. Relax the emotions. Let yourself become a little detached from the mind. You can do all this by simply focusing on your breath. As you breathe in, breathe in consciously. You are breathing in spiritual energy. As you breathe out, let go of all tensions, worries, and concerns. As your breathing slows down, the body begins to relax. The tight muscles start relaxing and letting go. As the muscles let go, the pain begins to release. You start to feel good. You start to feel God.

In that feeling of uplifting joy, begin to image-in (imagine) that you have a brand new start as of right now. It doesn't matter how old your physical body is. It doesn't matter whether you're male or female. This energy is not prejudiced on any level. It lets you do as you please. If you do good things, you will attract good things to you. If you do bad things (if there are such things), you will attract that to you.

There is a challenge in this world to hold in your mind only images of what you want. Like attracts like. Misery loves company. If you are miserable, you will attract other miserable people to you. Many people are looking for any excuse to complain. That justifies their existence. Perhaps they feel they have to justify their existence. In truth, simply being here is justification enough.

You don't have to prove anything to anybody. You don't have to prove you're here. You don't have to hold up images for people to look at. You don't have to try to be something you're not. Stop holding up images; let others get a good look at the real you. If they like you, you're in. If they don't, you can save yourself from playing all the games that you would have ultimately lost anyway.

You can get out of any space that is not working for you. You can actually change your inner consciousness by going on what we call the *mental diet*. What is the mental diet? For 30 days, entertain only positive thoughts. Do not purposefully take negative thoughts inside you; do not hold them in your mind or go over and over them. If a negative thought does come into your mind, immediately change the imagery from negative to positive, and let the thought go. Don't dwell on anything negative.

Does this mean you should be oblivious to something that is going on around you? I didn't say you were supposed to be stupid. If you see something negative, look at it and, if you can, change it. If it is your area of concern, handle it. If it's not, move from it so that those equipped for it can handle it. That's being smart.

You are responsible for what you hold in your mind, not for what goes through it. You may say, "But there's a serious illness in my family. How do I *not* hold a negative thought about the illness?" I didn't say it would be easy. It can be quite a challenge.

Here's one way to get rid of illness in the family. Hold

in your consciousness a picture of that person's health, wealth, and happiness. See the person well and vital, walking around, and enjoying the family. If you do it strongly enough, along with getting appropriate medical care, the person can improve on many levels.

You might say, "But they are so far gone; I doubt that anything can be done. They are senile and unconscious most of the time." Even then there is no need for you to worry. If your positive thoughts, your prayers, and your mental imagery of the person's health won't bring it forth, it is certain that your worry and despair won't, either. It may be time to prepare the rest of the family for the time when that person is gone. This is reality. You do what you can do, and when you can do no more, you let it go. No matter what the situation, worrying won't accomplish anything useful.

A psychiatrist once told me, "You can only help people so much; then you have to stand back. If they won't do it by themselves, you have to hospitalize them or put them into an environment where people are trained to look after their needs." Families often think, "Oh no, I couldn't put my loved one into a hospital." The family, however, may not be trained, prepared, or equipped to take care of the one who is ill.

When you can do no more for people physically, inwardly hold a picture of them being happy until they leave the physical body. Then envision them at the highest level of consciousness that you know. Don't hold them back with your grief. Help them on with your love. Don't deny them a chance for that last minute of peace and contentment.

If you have been holding only positive thoughts, when someone you know dies, you'll be clear. You won't have to live in remorse, regret, or guilt. While people are here, demonstrate your love for them. Ask them what you can do for them. If they say they are content and not lacking anything, believe them and let it go.

Acceptance and love will release the locks that have been put in the subconscious mind. Sometimes subconscious blocks can be released by confronting them even if you don't know their origins. For example, let's say that you just don't like the color yellow; it irritates and upsets you. You don't want anything to do with yellow. You won't go into a yellow room, you won't eat lemons, and you won't ride in a yellow taxicab. You may not remember the movie, the rain, or the yellow parking ticket the attendant gave you. It's not necessary to remember the incident in order to break the pattern. You break it by confronting it.

Go into the theater of the mind and see yourself entering into these situations that you would normally avoid. Hold the image of success in your mind. See yourself feeling good about standing in a yellow room, and hear yourself saying, "It's just another color."

The next time someone asks if you'd like some lemon in your tea, say, "Okay." Squeeze it yourself. Tell yourself, "It's okay; it's just a lemon."

Suppose you have yellow rooms and lemons handled, but you still don't like yellow taxicabs. You still won't get in one. Go back into the theater of the mind. See yourself calling a yellow taxicab. See yourself getting in. You may say, "Wait a minute. I got as far as envisioning myself opening the cab door, and now I'm shaking inside." Open your eyes. It is only an exercise of the mind. There is no taxicab present. You can relax.

It's possible to get wrapped up in your mind because this level is extremely powerful. If the process of envisioning gets too intense, open your eyes and reestablish where you are and what's happening. Then try it again. Close your eyes and see the taxicab again. Open the door and start to get in. If it feels a bit rough, remember that it's only in your mind. There's no meter running, so you can take all the time you want.

When you feel you can handle it, get all the way in the taxicab and close the door. Take a ride around the block. That may be all that you can handle at this time, but you have succeeded. You have broken the block of *yellow*, and since that is accomplished, the blocks of the movie, the rain, the windshield wipers, the song on the radio, and the parking lot attendant will start breaking. They were all connected. When you break one, you break them all.

The creative nature of God is inside you. You take the energy in, one breath at a time, and with that energy you set up a pattern. Sometimes you create a mess. Sometimes you create beauty. The God in you is learning to know itself by its own creation. The supreme God is the God of love, the God of infinite patience that says, "You can take as long as you like to work your energy. I'm going to be here when you turn to the consciousness of love."

Love and affection are two different things. In affection, you can get hurt. You can get hurt when you give only 50 percent. You can get hurt when you give 99 percent. When you give 100 percent, you are demonstrating perfection, and you cannot be hurt in perfection.

You may say, "That sounds real good, but. . . ." What is the *but*? What is your block? Did someone once turn you down so that now you have that rejection locked into the reactive mind? Get it out. Release it.

Why did the person turn you down? Bad breath? Dandruff? Weren't you standing close enough to your shower? The point is, was it *you* that they rejected or was it something you were doing that you could change? Even when you have changed, the person might say, "But now I have someone else." Don't worry. You'll get another chance—not necessarily with that person, but with someone.

Many people are looking for someone to lift them, to take care of them, and to share with them—not in a smothering or mothering way, but as a lover. Being a lover means being in a consciousness that says, "No matter what you do, I still love you." It's the love of the parents who pour love into their baby. They probably don't love the dirty diapers, but they get in there and clean up the mess anyway. That is part of their responsibility as creators. It's called spiritual ecology. Until a child is old enough to take care of itself, somebody must do it for them.

The baby cries out from its beingness, "Love me." Who can deny that call of love? I've seen tough men, bankers and financial experts whose primary reality is dollars and cents, look at a baby and melt inside. Then they check to see if anyone saw them. If someone did, they excuse it by saying, "It must have been something I ate." It was not something they ate. It was love. It cannot be denied.

Some people think the spiritual path is easy. It's not; it's hard. The weak don't make it. On the spiritual path, you must walk to the beat of your own drummer and do for yourself the things that work for you. You have to please yourself. (If you don't, that is your damnation, and it can be difficult.) Do you really have any other choice? No, because the spiritual consciousness is flooding this entire planet.

I've been around the world several times and have seen all sorts of people—young, old, rich, poor, happy, desperate—and I have found that when you put a smile on your face, you speak a universal language. The love in your heart comes right out and gives to others.

I've had strangers come up to me and share things that are personal and beautiful. It sometimes startles me because this isn't the way people usually do things. People often ignore one another's presence because they're afraid the other is after something they don't want to give. If you can't give of yourself, no one else can give to you. No one can help you.

If you bump into a wall and turn around and *ask* for help, I'll be glad to do what I can for you. I'll be glad to point out where the door is. I can point the way to a lot of places for a lot of people. Unless you do something for yourself, however, my advice won't mean much. Wishing won't do it. Hoping won't do it. Wishing and hoping are negative faith. The way to get something done is to *do it.*

Through truth, you gain freedom. The truth is what works for you. It may appear to change from time to time, but truth should be your experience, your life. It's easier to agree on the negative than to agree on the positive. To do that, you must give up your point of view, your conditioning, your prejudice, your ego and say, "Father-Mother-God, Thy will is done."

God's will *is* done, whether you like it or not. When you fight against it, you position yourself in negativity. When you attempt to work your will as closely as possible to the will of Spirit, you are working toward the positive. When your will and the will of Spirit match, you are filled to overflowing. You know that God is in heaven and all is right with the world. You don't feel separated or lost. You don't feel misused or abused. Used, yes! Everyone is here to be used. When you are doing God's will, you are the most useful to Spirit.

If you don't feel useful, at least you can be ornamental and pleasant to look at. If you can't say good things, at least don't add more garbage to what's already present. You can change these conditioned patterns of energy by getting to know your inner levels, those parts that are blocked and those parts that are overextended. Then you start balancing them by watching what you do, step by step.

Watching carefully what you do may sound difficult, but when you're more careful about what you put out, you get less back to handle. Then things get easier. As soon as you start this process, you'll find out what I'm talking about. You'll wonder why you delayed.

Many times in the past you have said, "I've made up my mind; I'm going to do this." You have placed it in the subconscious and in the universal mind, and you have willed it into being. In a week or so, however, you're no longer sure that is what you truly want. What happens to your programming? Your computer says, "Cancel." Then four days later you think, "I guess I do want that after all," and you activate it again. Then six days later, it's "cancel" again.

You might as well go back and start over. When you keep changing your decisions, your computer goes haywire and says, "Reject, reject, reject." Then you start feeling rejected. You ask, "Why do these things happen? Why don't good things come my way?" Why don't you *make up your mind* and stick to it? You might say, "I would if I could find it." Then make up your emotions. They're in your stomach, where you feel "butterflies." You make up your emotions by watching your breathing, becoming calm and relaxed, and feeling good. *Then* you check up on the mind.

The Bible says that as a man "thinketh in his heart, so is he" (Proverbs 23:7). The images that you hold in your consciousness are what you become. Do you know that many of the things that you hold in your mind aren't even yours? It's good to sort out what is and what isn't part of you and to get rid of that which isn't yours. Then you can decide what you want. Get your mind clear of your parents' wishes, your teachers' desires. and your ministers' points of view. Hold in your mind only that which you want more of.

Become highly selective and discerning about the thoughts that come into your mind. Observe your mind. Who is it that observes? You. You are not your mind, your emotions, or your body. Did you think you were? That is what has been conditioned into you through all the ads, television shows, magazines, and books that say, "Your beautiful body is all that's important." While that is all very fine, you might want to be selective about what you look at and what you bring into yourself.

The subconscious mind records even when you shut your eyes. It records what you hear; it records what you don't consciously hear. It's your recording mechanism. It records through your body, your emotions, and your mind. Be careful how you use it. Select the music you like to hear. Select your own rhythm. Don't expect someone else to like your rhythm all the time. Don't expect to like other people's rhythms all the time.

You *can* love everyone. You can sense love; you can feel love. You can perceive sincerity and honesty. The best check is to see what works for you. If it works, you don't have to be concerned whether someone else is telling the truth. It won't matter because it's working for you.

You know God by the unending presence of joy and love that spontaneously flows out. Even when you tell someone, "Look, you really bother me; would you mind going away?" you immediately add, "But not too far away. I love you no matter what, so go ahead and bother me anyway." If you love others enough, they can't bother you too long. Enough love overcomes all things.

Unconditional love allows perfect freedom. When a child falls while learning to walk, the parents don't rush over and say, "Never try to walk again; you might hurt yourself." They say, "Get up." The child gets up and falls again, and the parents say, "Get up again." They help the child as many times as necessary.

The child may fall and hit its head on the edge of the table. We've all done this. The child learns to watch for the edge of the table. You can't stop the child's experience of learning, but you can cushion the edge of the table. You can make it easier for the child.

Parents teach their children love, discipline, freedom, and upliftment by demonstrating these qualities in their own lives. Then the children won't have to play mother and father to themselves while they are growing up, and they won't have to play child to themselves or their spouses later on. They can grow into mature adults who understand the different levels of responsibility. When they would prefer not to do something they know must be done, they have the inner discipline and the inner freedom to do it anyway.

There is a difference between those who are progressing on the spiritual path and those who are letting their desires overcome them. Even in the midst of desire, the spiritual person says, "No, I won't give in to that because I know what the result will be. I will continue with what is working for me. I will maintain my center." Everyone has that ability. Some people demonstrate it more fully than others.

CHAPTER V

THE
POWER OF
YOUR
UNCONSCIOUS

W̶e sometimes deal with particular types of symbology within our consciousness, which set up forms of superstitious behavior. For example: if you see a falling star, make a wish; if you walk under a ladder, you'll have bad luck; if you step on a crack, you'll break your mother's back; if you get to the end of the street before the light changes, you'll get a date for tonight. These superstitious formations are held in the consciousness because of unresolved conflicts and the symbology in the unconscious mind.

Some interesting manifestations of unconscious symbology can be found in the game of baseball. For instance, Babe Ruth (who was originally a pitcher) would stick his tongue out every time he was going to throw a fast ball straight down the middle. Before long the rival teams had become aware of this, and their batters would get a hit time after time.

Someone finally held a mirror for Babe Ruth and said, "Now throw it straight down the middle." As he threw the ball, the Babe saw himself stick out his tongue. He said, "I didn't know I did that." From then on, he kept his tongue in his mouth. This was an unconscious pattern. Once he became aware of the pattern, he could change it.

Another way of approaching the unconscious level is through the use of symbology in the superstitious form: astrology, numerology, palmistry, tea-leaf reading, crystal ball gazing (scrying), mirror reading, and so forth. In all of these processes, you are dealing with symbols and forms and letting them reflect to you. You are dealing with a form of knowing (not intuition) in which you have a conviction of validity without an independent reference point. Some people call it seat-of-the-pants thinking; you move toward something just because it feels right. This is different from armchair philosophy, where you sit and think through various ideas to a logical conclusion.

When you work in the area of the occult, many unconscious patterns and symbols start coming up. As these appear, it may be difficult to tell what is actually going on. As you tap into these areas, your behavior may become erratic or appear neurotic; you may experience delusions of grandeur. The psychotic syndrome can be triggered when these unconscious patterns surface. There is no reference point in the conscious mind for these symbols and patterns; the mind cannot easily classify or categorize them. They just come flying up.

It is crucial to avoid dwelling on and delving into the occult levels unless you can cap these energies as they surface. If you can't, you may have to go to behavioral scientists, social workers, or institutions for medical and psychiatric therapy. The occult level should be approached only from a solid foundation combining the scientific, spiritual, and intuitive levels. People rarely seem to work that way, however. More often than not, the scientific, occult, and spiritual levels are seen as different and disassociated from one another.

When we use the conscious word-level to talk about the unconscious, we immediately start to misrepresent it. The only true way to communicate in the unconscious is unconsciously. This may sound like double-talk, but it isn't. While the unconscious is another aspect of our consciousness, it is a level of which we are completely unaware. Even our attempt to label it "unconscious" is an error in approach because labeling is a conscious process, and we have no way of being consciously aware of the unconscious.

You can know that which is unconscious through your unconscious mind. The key is to maintain the unconscious level so that you can bring your awareness there without interference. You cannot bring your mind, emotions, imagination, or body into the unconscious level; rather, you must simply float in a neutral manner through that level and accept whatever comes forward.

Traveling in the unconscious is not easily accomplished through meditation. It can be done through contemplation, however. Contemplation involves observing an object and letting it reveal to you what is there. The object does nothing; the observing of it allows the mind, imagination, and emotions to become still. Gradually, everything seems to go out of focus. When there is no focus, the unconscious levels start moving up.

As these unconscious levels surface, many things can be released. If there are repositories of illness, you may experience forms of memory in which you might say, "Oh yes, I remember hurting my shoulder years ago; it hurts again now, but not as badly." These are release patterns that are coming up. When you allow these releases and clearings to unfold naturally, you will experience very little difficulty. They will come forward only as you are able to understand and handle them.

Many things may be brought forward by accessing the unconscious through a psychic reader. The psychic, however, may be unaware of the unconscious level. They may be coming out of the mental level or the emotional level, and they may be able to make you feel good with an emotional interpretation of your unconscious symbology. Psychics may unlock the unconscious level for you, and you may walk away feeling good about them. Later on, however, these symbology levels from your unconscious may start kicking up other energies that aren't too pleasant.

If this happens you may go back to the psychic reader and say, "I have been having difficulties." The psychic may say, "That's interesting. You shouldn't be having any difficulties. When I gave you the reading, it felt very good to me." In their mind they may be saying, "But I said everything correctly." From their level of awareness, everything feels fine. Feelings often betray, however, and the mind doesn't know the unconscious. These psychics don't realize that they are releasing energies from a subtle level of which they are entirely unaware.

I know many people who have gone to various psychic readers and who have later come to me for a consultation. All I have done for an hour or more is cap the energies that have been unlocked during the psychic reading. This is necessary because the person is demonstrating that they are unable to handle the patterns that are coming forward.

Too often, I get the energies capped and contained only to have the person go back to the psychic reader and allow these unconscious energies to be unlocked again. The person may end up in a mental institution if this pattern continues. These psychic readers may like to think they are doing good, but they are actually doing great harm.

People often think that they are good at reading other people's symbology when they are actually reading out of their own levels of superstitious unconsciousness. It has been said, "When a pickpocket looks at a saint, he sees a pickpocket." Alcoholics see alcoholics. God sees God. The unconscious sees the unconscious.

It is important, when looking at the different levels of consciousness, to see them in a horizontal continuum rather than a vertical hierarchy. That way, you don't have to classify something as being better or worse than anything else; things are simply what they are. You approach each level in a matter-of-fact way.

You don't need anyone else to read your symbology for you. You don't need any interpretation of meanings. You may think, "Oh, God, I have this thing inside me that just keeps coming up. I hear it; I see it as a symbol in my mind; it's always here. What is it?" The answer is, "It doesn't matter. There is no way to know." You ask, "What can I do with it?" The answer is, "Nothing." You ask, "How can I get rid of it?" The answer is, "Get busy and do something physical; that will resolve the dilemma."

Take your unconscious dilemma, the superstitious haranguing you do, and run down the street with it. Physical exercise will do wonders toward relieving and resolving many emotional, mental, and unconscious dilemmas. People say, "I know I need more exercise, but running doesn't do it for me; it isn't the type of exercise I need." I have news for you—if you run long and hard enough, you won't need any other exercise. That will do it for you. Walking fast can also do it, as long as you keep moving and don't stop.

One way the unconscious influences us is through the formation of attitudes. People often ask, "What is an attitude? How do I get an attitude?" The unconscious level that we are working with is an important factor in determining our attitudes. Let's look at some of the dynamics in this process.

When youngsters are born, the unconscious is one of the first levels they express. Later they become aware of touch and taste. They are dealing in sensation, excitation, and stimulation. For a while the consciousness is fairly barren. It has a repository on hand, but that repository is not going to be tapped for a long time. Children first need to learn to use their muscles to perform in the physical world. This is their main job for a good many years.

As children get older, their attitudes begin to form through the process of looking at something and thinking about it. As they look and think, that thing becomes familiar. In that familiarity, they identify with it, and in the identification they say, "That is mine." If asked why it is theirs, their only reason may be that they have seen it a lot, and, therefore, it is theirs. Into the mind has come a feeling of ownership. This feeling is propped up with a value attitude that equates *mine* with *good* and that says, "This is mine is good is mine is good. . . ." It becomes a cycle of possessiveness.

It is wise to reevaluate your attitudes often. One way to do this is to focus inward for a time, closing your eyes so that you stop looking out. By shifting your focus away from your dilemma or problem, you can break the influence of the unconscious and change the attitude.

When you enter into the etheric level of your consciousness, it will make little sense to you because nothing is there except symbols. You must be careful not to look through the astral (imaginative) consciousness, see flying saucers, witches on broomsticks, or similar things, and think that because you have seen them with your imagination they actually exist. Often they do not; it is only projective imagery that you are dealing with. They may seem very real, but they are illusions.

Is this to say that these things can't exist? If you are talking about nuts-and-bolts proof, there is little evidence of their existence. People who are living in the consciousness of witches, demons, and flying saucers are living that reality, however. Society often looks upon these people as the fringe element.

It is best to be careful in these areas. While it can be interesting to see the symbology, the images, and the illusions, it is important to observe them as you would a painting on the wall: look at it and then go about your business. There isn't much usable reality there; it's only a symbolic representation.

Painting has become part of the great symbology of our time. When modern abstract art was popular, people were determining the value of a painting based on the symbology that would arouse itself out of the unconscious. They would buy the art based upon that.

After a while, however, there was so much of this type of art around that people began to feel overwhelmed by it. So abstract painting has diminished in popularity, and people are again looking for images that are solid and real. The old classical type of painting is popular again—landscapes, still lifes, and people who look like people.

Sculpture is still expressing a more abstract point of view. Many people who delight in this symbology go to all sorts of showings just to get aroused in this unconscious level.

The unconscious can sometimes be like a ferocious tiger, however, and can set loose strange vibratory frequencies in people. When this occurs, there can be a shift in attitude and in consciousness. Then these people may start manifesting their unconscious dilemma in the physical world as an art form or a certain behavior.

Another aspect of the unconscious can manifest in dancing. I once observed a most interesting example of this in a record store. There was music playing, what you might call hard rock or acid rock. A little girl about three years old started dancing. The more she got into it, the more she looked just like a penguin. That penguin symbology stayed with me quite a while.

Another time, I saw a television show of youngsters who were dancing to rock music. I looked for the symbology they were expressing. It was absolutely amazing. They were using a cathartic approach, but, at the same time, they were unlocking energies from the unconscious without knowing how to cap or hold them. As a result, they may enter into weird or antisocial behavior sometime in the future.

Naturally, not all of these youngsters will experience these behavior changes. They were dealing in an unknowing way with powerful energies, however, and they were certainly leaving themselves open to this possibility. Some of them may have to be institutionalized—not because there is anything habitually wrong with them, but because these frequencies are moving inside them. They tap into that energy, and then the energy starts to take over. There is no place to handle it in this world, so they start expressing bizarre behavior. They may laugh, giggle, talk nonsense, and in other ways express themselves in a manner unintelligible to the rest of the world. To them it is real; to the rest of us, it's crazy. They are actually out of balance—out of balance with their own form, which is peace and harmony.

The human consciousness has a natural rhythm and pace at which it evolves. In its own proper timing, it comes into greater and greater realizations about its true nature. It is designed to evolve into self-realization and awareness of God. Artificial attempts to speed up this process often result in delay and digression.

In your path toward self-awareness and God-awareness, it is best to select the natural methods of meditation, contemplation, spiritual exercises, study with enlightened teachers, and association with others who are also on the path of spiritual awareness. Your progress will be smoother and faster when you avoid the so-called short cuts.

There is a natural way to progress, and there are ways that attempt to control and manipulate life. We can look at this in terms of masculine and feminine polarities. The masculine attempts to control and direct his empire. He always strives to be in a superior position. The feminine doesn't have to do any of this because she is flowing in more of a natural harmony with everything around. There is no need for rules, regulations, or power struggles.

We need to blend the best of the masculine and feminine consciousnesses and come into a neutral balance in which we can maintain the power of our own self while we flow naturally with all things around us. Yes, it's ideal, and, yes, it's possible.

Nature progresses in a natural way, and nature's evolution includes the evolution of humankind. Some people ask, "What about the missing link?" There is no missing link. There are bridges from one race to another, and after the new race is established, there is no further need for the bridge.

On this planet, we are in a bridging race right now. At some point, races that are now on the planet will be gone. There will be no signs of them because this level will be pulled away. There will be nothing here to indicate that they were present. The new race will be present. We are not dealing here in terms of a few months or years, however, but thousands and thousands of years. Records of all this will be kept, of course, so there will be indicators of humankind's evolutionary progress.

Each person must be responsible for his or her total

beingness. This does not mean that we don't assist one another by scratching backs, getting a friend a glass of water, or giving someone a ride. It means all these things, as long as they are part of the flow of spiritual upliftment.

It's sometimes best not to give someone else the glass of water. Instead you say, "There is the water tap; there is the glass; help yourself." That approach can help people feel less dependent and more confident and able. We do this with youngsters so they can gain their own experience and increase their self-confidence.

Too often, when we gain a little spiritual knowledge, we want to grab people and lift them quickly. What happens, however, is that we grab them and trip them, and they fall. Then they become fearful of our approach to life.

Life is very natural, very simple. We make it complex by releasing energies within us through forms of symbology, through mentalizing, and through negative attitudes. These things create an inner struggle. We don't want the struggle, so we push it back into the unconscious. It struggles there and then manifests through illness or disease that our present sciences can neither identify nor clear. We can then find ourselves in a lot of physical trouble.

How can you handle these types of unconscious upheavals? You can practice spiritual techniques: meditations of various types, spiritual exercises, forms of contemplation, and mantras, as well as tones to focus, lift, and tie up the energies, giving them form so they flow more smoothly and you can feel more confident. There are techniques designed to reach into and clear many levels of consciousness. As you practice these spiritual techniques, you will become more familiar with the flow of energy within your consciousness, and you will feel more comfortable with yourself and others.

By continually working with the energies inside you,

you learn to recognize what they are—their purpose, their function, and their direction. You relax more into your be-ingness and bring forward a greater integration of all your levels. As this happens, you are no longer at the mercy of your physical habit-patterns, your emotional addictions, your mental games, or your unconscious urgings. You are able to direct yourself into more positive patterns of behavior and expression.

We evolve by going within and knowing all the levels with which we are involved. These levels are the physical body, the imagination, the emotions, the mind, the un-conscious, and the Soul. When we have established the awareness within, we can move to the outer realms and become aware that the outer spiritual world aligns with the inner kingdom. At that point, we will understand what it is all about. That understanding will surpass everything and will bring peace and joy.

CHAPTER VI

THE
POWER
WITHIN YOU

A friend once said to me, "It scares me to think that I create my own reality, that I am responsible for everything in my life, including the negativity that I experience. I don't know if I can create my life well enough." He didn't need to be afraid. His error was envisioning the process of taking responsibility for his life as an overwhelming task. Actually, he was already successful at creating. He had clothes on his back, food in his stomach, a roof over his head, and loving companions at his side. That, in itself, is great success.

The very fact that you are here—alive, breathing, and circulating blood through your veins—indicates that you are able to create your life successfully. Remember that you have been creating your life all along. The process didn't start the moment you became aware of it; it's been going on from the beginning.

You don't have to make any radical changes in order to begin taking conscious responsibility for your life. Look at your life; ask yourself what is working for you and what is working against you. Do more of what is working for you and less of what is working against you. Explore new approaches that might work even better for you than those you are using now.

Watch your thoughts. In the Bible it says that as a man "thinketh in his heart, so is he" (Proverbs 23:7). Another way of saying this is "energy follows thought." The thoughts that you hold in your consciousness will manifest for you in a number of different ways. If you want something and think about it a lot, your thoughts will be recorded in the universal mind, and the process of manifestation will be put in motion. That's one reason why we say, "Watch what you ask for; you just might get it."

The process works just the same if you *don't* want something and think about *that* a lot. The universal mind sees only the content and energy of your thoughts. Whatever you hold in your mind, positive or negative, the universal mind will attempt to supply for you. Therefore, it often happens that what you fear, you bring to you.

Concentrate on what you want; focus on that which will bring more loving and joy into your life. When you focus on the positive, you win in more ways than one. First, you are creating and promoting more positivity in your life. The more you focus on loving, the more loving you will draw to you. You are also enjoying a consciousness of loving here and now. If you want to be loving later, why not be loving now? As a matter of fact, the best way to ensure a positive future is to be positive in the present.

Watch your emotions. Emotions give energy to your thoughts and imagination. Putting emotion on a negative thought-pattern can give it the energy to cycle continually through your consciousness, bringing more negativity to you. A good rule of thumb is, for every feeling, have a thought to match it that you can act on physically in a positive way. This process allows you to harness the energy of your emotions to work for you, enhancing the quality of your life.

Watch what you do with your imagination. What pictures do you show yourself? What stories do you tell yourself? Use your imagination to line up your thoughts and feelings in a positive direction. Use the theater of the mind to clearly visualize your desired result.

Always win in your imagination. If you are telling yourself a story in which you lose, in which events turn against you, rewrite the ending. If you've made a mistake at work and you're imagining yourself being fired, change the script. See a new and better job opening up because you are free of the old job, or (if you like your job) see yourself creating a way to capitalize on your mistake in such a way that the whole company benefits and you get a raise in pay. That's the way to create your reality.

Ultimately, everything is perfect already. God's will is being done perfectly. You do have choices in this life, however, and the choices you make can affect the way you experience your life. If you choose to be happy, you will experience happiness. If you choose to be depressed, you will experience depression. It's your choice.

You might ask, "What if I'm already depressed? I can't just choose to be happy and make it so." Have you ever been depressed at one time, and then happy later on? At some point you chose to let go of your depression, and at some point you chose to be happy again. If you're going to be happy later, why not be happy now? If you're going to be loving later, why not be loving now?

Everything in your life is a reflection of what you have created, allowed, or promoted at some time. Take what you have, and use it to build the life you want. Tend your life as you would a garden. Weed out those things you no longer want or need, and nurture with loving care those things you value. Also take the time to stand back from your life and to see it in the larger context. Take the time to go inside, where the outer distractions won't hinder your view of who you really are.

We bring to ourselves that which we focus upon, so it makes sense to focus upon the best, the highest thing we know. If your goal is to awaken to the truth of who you really are, then focus on that truth as you know it. As you focus on it, it will reveal itself to you.

There is an ancient phrase I use—Baruch Bashan—that means "the blessings already are." Knowing that we create our own lives can be one of our greatest blessings. It is our key to freedom on this level. Nothing that you did or that was done to you can stop you from achieving your destiny. Take the tools given to you and use them wisely to create your outer life in such a way that it reflects your inner majesty.

When your inner and outer realities truly match, you will be home free, living your destiny as a co-creator with God. Remember that not one Soul is ever lost, that God loves all of Its creation, and that you are never given more than you can handle. Love your life—yourself—as God loves you and you will never feel lost. You will know that everything that comes to you is to lift you. As this loving fills your heart, you will know that, indeed, the blessings already are.

ABOUT THE AUTHOR

John-Roger is the founder and current spiritual director of the Movement of Spiritual Inner Awareness. He brings to his work an educational background in psychology and over 20 years of counseling, teaching, writing, and speaking. Most important, he shares from his experience and can assist others in awakening to their own connection to Spirit.

Like many of us, John-Roger began his journey long before he knew about it himself. It wasn't until a serious accident in 1963, when he had a near-death experience, that he had a startling transformation of consciousness. At that time, John-Roger became what many would call self-realized, yet it was something more. His awakened self led him into a life of service and, more significantly, a path of loving. This consciousness of unconditional loving that he manifests became known as the Mystical Traveler Consciousness.

In explaining what this consciousness is, John-Roger has said that "the nature of the Mystical Traveler is love, joy, and upliftment. It brings health, wealth, and happiness on the physical level, calm to the emotional level, peace to the mental level, ability to the unconscious level, and fulfillment to the spiritual level by awakening the divine heritage in each person."

In addition to his role as founder and spiritual director of MSIA, John-Roger is also founder of Prana Theological Seminary and College of Philosophy, a school for spiritual studies; the Heartfelt Foundation, dedicated to community service; Baraka Center, a holistic healing and research clinic; Insight Transformational Seminars, offering a range of personal growth seminars; Koh-E-Nor University, a fully approved, degree-granting university; Integrity Foundation, dedicated to promoting personal integrity; and the John-Roger Foundation, sponsor of the International Integrity Award. The JRF is also the flagship organization that provides support to the above organizations as well as to other groups and individuals involved with education, health, science, research, community service, and the study of individual and world peace.

For further information, contact
MSIA,® P.O. Box 3935, Los Angeles, CA 90051